An Unpopular Guide
to
Step 5

by

Several Program Members

Revised with the assistance of
CA, DD, RD, GG, and NV
Thank you

Quotations from the book *Alcoholics Anonymous* are taken from the First and
Second Editions, whose copyright has expired in the USA. For copyright reasons,
this work should not be distributed outside the United States of America

Further paperback copies of this book can be ordered on-line at
https://www.createspace.com/4098583

Version 0.121214

A Note

This *Unpopular Guide to Step 5* is intended to be available free from on-line resources. E-book versions or printed versions may also be available or may become available. Where there is a charge for these e-book or printed versions, that charge should cover only the cost of creating, printing, and/or hosting those versions. No royalty payments or other payments of any description are made to the writers of this *Guide*.

About the Unpopular Books and Guides

Why is this series of books and guides called "Unpopular"?

The so-called Big Book of the fellowship of Alcoholics Anonymous is the basis for recovery for countless millions of people around the world. The reason for this is that the Big Book "show[s] other alcoholics precisely how we have recovered" and offers "clear-cut directions ... showing how we recovered." Consequently, most of us follow its recommendations closely.

But for some reason, certain sections of the Big Book – just as explicit as other sections – are generally ignored. Not only that: when it is pointed out that they are being ignored, the reaction of many people in recovery can range from bewilderment to hostility.

Mainly, therefore, these books and guides focus on those neglected sections of the Big Book ... however unpopular they (and we) may be.

Introduction

Step 5: Admitted to God, to ourselves, and to another human being the exact nature of our wrongs

An Unpopular Guide to Step 5 has two potential audiences.

The first is those members of Program who may not yet have undertaken Step 5.

The other potential audience is people comprising the vast majority in Program: that is, those of us who have already completed Step 5 by reading our Step 4 inventory to another person – *even though the Big Book of Alcoholics Anonymous makes no mention at all of such a practice.*

Now, this is very odd. It's odd because – as we are frequently reminded in meetings of AA and other 12-Step fellowships – the Foreword to the First Edition of the Big Book says that its main purpose is to show "other alcoholics *precisely how we have recovered*" (italics in the original). On page 29 of the Big Book, we read, "[C]lear-cut directions are given showing how we recovered." We have all met and listened to the so-called "Big Book thumpers" in 12-Step meetings – those members who insist on a literal following of the suggestions in the book. Perhaps we ourselves are "Big Book thumpers." Why is it that these book-thumpers don't "thump" the treatment of Step 5 in pages 72-75 of the Big Book?

We cannot know *why* countless members of Program have done their Step 5 – and have advised others to do Step 5 – by simply reading the contents of their Step 4 inventory. At some time or another this practice began, and we may suppose that it will continue into the future. But this is not how the Big Book suggests we undertake Step 5.

Part of the intent of this *Guide,* therefore, is to explore what the Big Book actually says with regard to our working of Step 5.

But there is another motive in writing *An Unpopular Guide to Step 5.* It is to understand *why* the Big Book recommends that Step 5 should be a telling of our "whole life story" rather than the reading of our Step 4 inventory. We will see that there is a very intimate connection between such an approach and our working of Step 10. When we see the reason for the Big Book's treatment of Step 5, it may be that we become more inclined to follow its suggestions … and, just as important, to recommend to newcomers to Program that they do the same.

As ever, we ask that you take what you can use and leave the rest behind. But we hope that, as a result of reading what we have to say, some of us in recovery will begin to explore the very real benefits of working Step 5 the way that we are told the first one hundred members of AA worked it.

What we will be talking about

To show other alcoholics precisely how we have recovered is the main purpose of this book.

-- Big Book,
Foreword to the First Edition

[C]lear-cut directions are given showing how we recovered.

-- Big Book, page 29

We will be talking about the following topics in the Big Book's treatment of Step 5:

1. The story
2. The discussion
3. Step 5, Step 10, and Step 11
4. Our Higher Power

We'll finish by drawing some conclusions from these topics.

1. The story

*[T]hey had not learned enough of humility, fearlessness and honesty, in the sense we find it necessary, until they told someone else all their life **story** .... Such parts of our **story** we tell to someone who will understand, yet be unaffected .... When we decide who is to hear our **story**, we waste no time ....*

--Big Book, pp.73-75

Stories have always been important in 12-Step recovery programs.

The first edition of the Big Book of the fellowship Alcoholics Anonymous contained several stories about individual recovery. The reason for this is quite simple. It was done primarily because it was intended that the *book itself* be the means of recovery. The Big Book was written for people who might remain forever beyond the reach of other members of Program and who would therefore have to attain sobriety alone. To help these readers of the Big Book, who might have no one else to talk to about the problem of alcoholism and how to recover from it, the book included a set of stories.

As it turned out, the fellowship expanded faster than anyone could have imagined. AA meetings sprang up all over the USA and then all over the world. But nevertheless, the tradition of including stories was retained in subsequent editions of the Big Book.

But we do not encounter stories only in the Big Book. We also listen to them in AA meetings and meetings of other 12-Step based fellowships. We retain the practice of having "speaker meetings," where a member shares his or her "experience, strength, and hope" with other members of that particular program. In other words, that member shares his or her story of recovery. And the various conventions that our different fellowships have from time to time almost always focus strongly on talks by speakers – sometimes so-called "circuit speakers" – who share the story of how they recovered.

But the telling of stories is of course many thousands of years older than any 12-Step program. Most of us love stories. We are told stories when we are children. We continue to read stories and enjoy them as we get older. We tell stories, or listen to stories, about the countries we belong to, the religious movements we belong to, even the families we belong to. These stories help us to feel that we belong.

Very broadly, there are two kinds of stories we can tell.

There are fictional stories: stories which are clearly made up, told to entertain or to frighten, to explain (for example, myths) or to comfort.

And – at the other end of the scale – are stories which we believe are "true" rather than fictional – stories such as the Revolutionary War in the United States, or the rise of the trades unions in nineteenth-century England, or the migration of early humans out of Africa into the European land-mass.

We think that we understand very clearly the difference between these two kinds of stories. And yet, when we begin to look at them, we see that it is sometimes very difficult to determine which stories are fictional and which are "real."

For example, Christians who are creationists may regard the creation "myths" found in the Book of Genesis in the Bible as literally true, while they simultaneously view the so-called "scientific" explanation as a fabrication. Meanwhile, Christians who believe in the "facts" of science claim that stories about evolution told by scientists are true, while the creation myths are "simply stories."

Another example: A popular modern writer wrote a best-selling account of America in which he pointed out that the Pilgrim Fathers contrived to arrive at Plymouth Rock in the *Mayflower* with no agricultural implements, and a general lack of preparedness which would probably have resulted in their deaths had it not been for the fact that one of the Indians could speak English. As a result of reiterating these historical facts, the writer received death threats from some American readers who viewed the Pilgrim Fathers in a very different light, as bringers of Western civilization to a spiritually benighted continent.

We learn something important from this confusion in people's minds about the stories that they tell, and the extent to which those stories may or may not be "true." We learn that we tend to have an emotional investment in the stories we tell one another. We learn that – the closer to home these stories are – the stronger that emotional investment is. For example, to this day there is a tendency to view the American Civil War differently if you live in Georgia than if you live in New York state, even though that war happened a century and a half ago.

The stories in which we have the strongest emotional investment are the stories we create about ourselves as individuals. These stories can be, and often are, very powerful. And the main source of that power is that *most of us are unaware of the fact that we have a story about ourselves to begin with.*

We have little or no awareness that we create stories about ourselves. We have little or no awareness that we take ownership of, and then attempt to persuade others of the truth of, our story.

Instead, we believe that certain things *happened* to us, most of them early in life, which definitively shaped us. And we believe that the connection between those things that happened and what we then became is a *fact.* We believe that we became addicted despite our best efforts, and we believe that this too is a *fact.* We can come up with a list of circumstances, people, and places which caused us to make bad choices in our life, and we believe that there was an inevitability to this "cause and effect," that it too is a *fact.* We see ourselves as the inevitable product or result of these external forces, and we see that too as a *fact.* All these things are *facts.* They are not parts of a story that we have made up about ourselves – oh no! They are *facts.*

When we have an emotional investment in a story, we tend to get upset or angry if someone suggests the story is not true. For example, if we believe that the United States has been overall a force for good in the world, and then we encounter someone who denies that this is the case, we can become defensive or angry with that person.

But the defensiveness and anger we may show there is nothing compared to the defensiveness or anger we showed around the stories we told about ourselves before we came to Program.

Before we came to Program, people would tell us to "pull ourselves together." They would say to us, "If you

really loved your children you'd stop drinking so much."
They would tell us, "If you had any self-respect you'd get
out of that abusive relationship ...." And when they did,
then we *really* got annoyed. How dare they say those
things! If those people only understood what we'd been
through ... if they only understood how destructive our
upbringing had been ... if they only understood that our
partner would probably *die* if we left him or her ... if they
only understood that the only way it was possible to live
with our family is if we humored that raging family
member ... *if they would only listen to and accept the
"facts" of our lives, then they would see that we had no
alternative but to keep living the lives we were living.*

As practicing addicts, when we encountered criticisms
such as these we found ourselves in a paradoxical
situation.

On the one hand, we believed that the forces arrayed
against us throughout our lives were *real*. The details of
our family lives, our work lives, the misery of poverty or
of emotional or other abuse were *facts*. They were not a
story: these things *really happened* and *really made us the
people we had become.*

On the other hand, we also found that – for some
mysterious reason – our critics seemed to be immune to
these facts. So we had to attempt to *sell* them on those
supposedly objective facts. We had to point out that they
simply didn't understand the reality of our situation. We
had to attempt to persuade them to our point of view. We
found ourselves in a peculiar position. On the one hand,
we *maintained that we didn't have a story* – that our critics
were for some reason refusing to acknowledge the *facts* of
our existence. On the other hand, we were *simultaneously*

trying to sell those critics on the story that we maintained we didn't have.

If there is one thing that addicts tend to be weak at, it's dealing with paradoxes like this. It was stressful to insist on the one hand that we were addicts through no fault of our own, and on the other hand to attempt to "sell" people on the reality of our situation. In fact, it was so stressful that it simply drove us further into the practice of our addiction. When an addict tries over and over to do these two opposing things, then one day he or she will reach rock-bottom. In fact, that is what "rock-bottom" actually is. It's a total collapse of our world, brought on by insisting on the truth of a story that we claim we don't have to begin with.

Reaching rock-bottom marks the end of telling that old story. When "we admitted that we were powerless over" our addiction "and that our lives had become unmanageable," our carefully crafted story disappeared ... and our recovery began.

When we came to Program, we encountered two important things.

The first was the need for honesty, particularly self-honesty: that honesty, in fact, which the AA Big Book insists in Chapter 5 is the one pre-requisite for recovery.

And we also encountered a group of people who came from backgrounds just like ours, sometimes down to the very details ... *but who told a completely different story about their lives from anything we had heard before.* Many of the *facts* of their addicted lives might be similar to the *facts* of our own lives. But the *stories* they told around those facts bore no resemblance to the story we had tried so hard to sell to other people. These were people who seemed to be able to accept that in some way they had *created* their addiction. They seemed willing to take responsibility for the poor decisions they had made in their lives, while acknowledging at the same time that they might have been treated very badly by other people. They seemed to find amusing certain episodes which were similar to the ones we had experienced. These episodes had caused us grief, humiliation, lack of self-respect, but our new friends in Program described them in very different terms. In fact, sometimes these new friends seemed to think that their humiliating experiences were *funny*.

In fact, the new kinds of stories we heard around the old experiences of this group of people were the gateway to Step 2 of our programs. We "came to believe that a Power greater than ourselves could restore us to sanity" because it seemed that these new friends had experienced that restoration. They did not deny the unpleasant, selfish and self-serving things that they had done. They did not pretend that other people had not treated them badly. But these same "facts" that had been the basis of our old, self-justifying story were now – for these new friends of ours – the raw material of a more positive, less self-pitying, and more *balanced* story. And as we heard these new stories that were being told by our new friends, we came to believe that perhaps the story we had been telling ourselves for all those years was untrue. We came to believe that we could tell a new story about ourselves, just as these new friends in recovery had managed to do.

As we learn our new story, we get on with the Steps. We take Step 3 as soon as we can. We commence our Fourth Step inventory. *And then we work Step 5 just as it suggests in the AA Big Book. We tell someone else our new story.*

What we need to do in Step 5, as soon as possible, is to tell our whole life story to someone *having first examined in detail in our Step 4 inventory just who we are, what we did, and the extent to which we were driven by fear and selfishness*. When we work Step 5 in this way, we have the opportunity *for the first time* to be completely open and honest with someone about our entire lives.

We are no longer trying to represent ourselves as hapless victims of our addiction, innocent individuals forced by other people, places and things into alcoholism, gambling, overeating, or subordinating ourselves to other people in our lives. Instead, as a result of our Step 4 inventory, we have determined for ourselves who we are. As the Big Book reminds us in its treatment of Step 3, we're a mixture. Our Step 4 inventory shows that sometimes we are cheats and liars; sometimes we are manipulators and compulsive martyrs; sometimes we are adulterers and thieves; sometimes we have been driven throughout our lives by selfishness and fear. Sometimes, on the other hand, we have been "kind, considerate, patient, generous; even modest and self-sacrificing" (this phrase is a direct quote from the Big Book). Almost always we have been driven by fear and selfishness. And it is this person – the person who was sometimes the cheat, the liar, the manipulator, the compulsive martyr, and sometimes the person who was kind and modest – who is going to take center-stage in the new story of ourselves that we are going to tell in Step 5.

Because we are now going to be able to tell a new story. It is going to be ultimately a story of hope, told by someone who has at last found the strength to look at him- or herself openly and honestly. It is going to be a story told to another individual with whom we are prepared to share everything about ourselves. For the first time in our lives we will not be telling our story in order to sell someone else on our point of view. We will be telling our story because we have had the courage and fortitude to look at ourselves unflinchingly in our Step 4 inventory. We are now ready to tell somebody else as honestly as we can what really happened in our lives.

2. The discussion

*This is perhaps difficult – especially **discussing** our defects with another person .... We will be more reconciled to **discussing** ourselves with another person when we see good reasons why we should do so ....[T]he great necessity for **discussing** ourselves with someone ....*

-- *Big Book, pp. 72-74*

Confess your faults, one to another.

-- *Epistle of James, 5:16*

To repeat what was said at the start of this Guide: Most of us have worked our Fifth Step by reading our written Fourth Step, usually to a sponsor.

But there is no mention of this practice in the Big Book. Indeed, in the whole of the treatment of Step 5, which can be found on pages 72-75, the paperwork we created in Step 4 is mentioned only once. On page 75, the Big Book says *When we decide who is to hear our story, we waste no time. We have a written inventory and we are prepared for a long talk.* That's the last time there is any mention of our written inventory in Step 5. The next time it's referred to is on page 76. That may not seem very far off, but it's far enough that the reference is in the context of working Step 8 – not Steps 6 or 7 and certainly not Step 5.

So there is but a single mention of our written inventory in Step 5. And even there, the Big Book merely says that we have our written inventory with us. There is no recommendation there or anywhere else in the Big Book that we should read that inventory out loud as part of our Step 5. Yet generations of recovering addicts and – perhaps more to be regretted – their sponsors have assumed the opposite: that the Big Book is recommending that Step 5 should consist of reading that written inventory.

As we noted, the written inventory is mentioned just *once*, almost in passing. By contrast, the framing of our Fifth Step as a *discussion* occurs **three times**. Our Fifth Step is characterized **three times** as the telling of our *story*. Since there is no overt mention at all of reading any written inventory, and since these words each appear three times, it would be reasonable to assume that the Big Book is recommending a "discussion" of our "story" with another person – not the reading of our written inventory to another person.

We have already talked about the role of our story in our recovery. In the previous chapter we tried to understand what the nature of this story is. We have seen that our story changes as we come into Program. Our old story, based on the supposed *facts* of our unhappy lives, is replaced with a new, honest, and more hopeful story. In this chapter we want to look at the idea of Step 5 as a discussion between two people (or possibly more: note the reference to "persons" at the top of page 74). Let's look carefully at the Big Book and see what it says about who these two people are.

One of these people is the recovering addict. Who is the other person? Is it our sponsor? Is it someone else in Program?

Well, the answer to both those questions is *no* – not necessarily. The word *sponsor* does not occur anywhere in the first 164 pages of the Big Book. So apparently it was possible, and is still possible, to have our Step 5 discussion with someone other than a sponsor. But the Big Book does even less than that. It does not even recommend that the other person be in Program.

So who or what exactly does the Big Book say that this other person *should* be?

The other person is described as "another human being," "another person," "someone else"; he or she is described as perhaps "the properly appointed authority whose duty it is to receive [confession]," possibly "someone ordained by an established religion." Or it may be "a close-mouthed, understanding friend." It might conceivably be "our doctor or psychologist," or even a family member, though this last possibility seems to be discouraged. The "right person" should be "able to keep a confidence" and should "fully understand and approve what we are driving at," it should be someone who "will not try to change our plan," someone who is "a partner," who will "realize that we are engaged upon a life-and-death errand."

Let's look at that list again. Clearly a priest or minister is suggested; a friend who understands and who will keep a confidence; a doctor or psychologist. If any of these people are acceptable, what is it that they have in common which would make them a good choice for our Step 5 discussion? As we look over the list again, the word that perhaps jumps out as much as any is the word *partner*.

Even though the list contains religious officials and medical professionals, the key idea seems to be that we are engaging in Step 5 with an *equal*. That person may or may not be a recovering addict: as we have already seen, the list is remarkable in that any mention of working our Fifth Step with another recovering addict is absent. Instead, what we undertake in Step 5 is done with the assistance of a partner. That partner should be someone who may be able to contribute to this "discussion" based on his or her professional or religious experience, or even someone who is a friend, who is "close-mouthed and understanding." In other words, the other party in a Step 5-based discussion need have no personal experience of having done a Fifth Step him- or herself, nor the experience of having participated in a Step 5-based discussion before. The recovering addict may consider it *desirable* that his or her discussion partner should have had those experiences, but they are not apparently *necessary*.

So what *is* necessary for our discussion partner?

One characteristic the people on that list appear to have in common is *wisdom:* the wisdom to listen carefully, to contribute from their own experience of life, to participate in a discussion *without succumbing to the temptation of telling the recovering addict what he or she should say, should reveal, or should do afterwards.*

And perhaps there is another characteristic we should add to the people on the list. They will be *humble.* Members of a religious group or of professional medical bodies routinely have church members or patients tell them things in complete confidence. They have the knowledge and training that enables them to know when they should merely listen. A close-mouthed, understanding friend may not have that knowledge and training, but that seems not to matter as long as he or she is wise and humble enough to listen, to contribute from his or her own experience, but never to tell the recovering addict what he or she should do.

Of course, as we look at this list of suggestions of people with whom the recovering addict might work his or her Fifth Step, it's important to remember the situation which the writing of the Big Book was intended to address. It's easy to forget that it was addressed to alcoholics who had never heard of the fledgling fellowship of Alcoholics Anonymous. It was addressed to people who wanted to do something about their alcoholism even though there might be no other alcoholics, recovering or otherwise, to help them. It was addressed to people who probably had no access to an AA group or an AA sponsor. We can be fairly sure that the list of potential "partners" with whom a Fifth Step could be undertaken reflects this fact. Those who wanted to recover by working the suggested program of twelve Steps needed to be able to share their whole life story with someone other than a fellow member of Program.

But clearly the writers of the Big Book believed that it was perfectly *possible* to have an effective discussion of our story with someone who was not a fellow-member. So the significance of the list of people, particularly the characteristics which those people have in common, retains its importance for us. It is those characteristics which make them suitable partners for our practice of Step 5.

Our Fifth Step, then, is not a reading of our written inventory. It does not have to be done with a sponsor. It does not even have to be done with someone in Program. It is a discussion that takes place with someone who can listen, someone with wisdom and humility, someone who can contribute to the discussion from his or her own experience – not necessarily of Program, but of life. And we are going to tell, and discuss, our whole life story with this person, armed with the insights about ourselves that we learned when we did Step 4.

Some of us are lucky enough to have experienced this practice of Step 5 – to have worked with someone in Program who had actually read what the Big Book says about Step 5, to have told that person our whole life story, to have had a discussion with that person. One of our number originally did his Fifth Step the "wrong" way, by reading his Step 4 inventory to his sponsor. Subsequently, he repeated those two Steps under the direction of a new sponsor – *a sponsor who had read and understood what the Big Book recommends about Step 5.* That Program member spent several hours on a long walk through the countryside with a sponsor who listened to his whole life story, who asked questions, who contributed insights from his own recovery. Our friend had his written inventory with him; but not until the very end of the day did he refer to it to see if there was anything important he had left out of his story.

Our friend has taken a long journey to the daily practice of the last three Steps in his recovery. Indeed, he would be the first to admit that that journey could have happened a great deal faster. But he dates his "true" recovery in Program from that day – the day he practiced Step 5 in just the way the Big Book recommended, by discussing his whole life story.

3. Step 5, Step 10, and Step 11

Continue to watch for selfishness, dishonesty, resentment, and fear. When these crop up, we ask God at once to remove them. We discuss them with someone immediately ....

-- Big Book, p.84

When we retire at night, we constructively review our day. Were we resentful, selfish, dishonest or afraid? Do we owe an apology? Have we kept something to ourselves which should be discussed with another person at once?

-- Big Book, p.86

As we have already mentioned, one of the odd features of the Big Book *Alcoholics Anonymous* is the fact that in its first 164 pages there is no mention of the word *sponsor*. And we have noted that one reason for its absence is the situation in which the Big Book was written. It was created within a few short years of the start of the fellowship itself. Indeed, we know that the number of alcoholics who were sober at the time of its appearance was about a hundred, and one or two of them were fairly shaky in their recovery. In other words, when the book was written it was still not too easy to distinguish the recovering alcoholics from the complete newcomers.

However, the writers of the Big Book clearly believed that it was possible to recover from alcoholism without the help of a sponsor. Indeed, there seems to be some suggestion that it was possible to recover without the help of another recovering alcoholic: this was the precise scenario that the book was designed to address. But it is also clear that the writers believed that *it was not possible to recover on one's own.* There would have to be help from other people. Presumably it would be best if those other people were members of the fellowship too ... *but they did not have to be.*

Bearing this in mind – the fact that the recovering alcoholic needed help from other people, but those other people did not have to be sponsors or even members of the fellowship of AA – let's look at the treatment of Step 10 and Step 11 in the Big Book. These are steps which – just like Step 5 – are best done with the help of someone else. In Step 5, as we have seen, we are offered a description of what that person should be like. We have read that the person to whom we tell our whole life story in Step 5, and with whom we discuss our whole life story, should be a wise, close-mouthed partner or equal. In other words, our Step 5 can be done with someone who meets these criteria, regardless of whether they are in Program.

We'll look first at Step 10, which urges us essentially to repeat the process of Steps 4 through 9 on a continuous, moment-by-moment basis. It says, *Continue to watch for selfishness, dishonesty, resentment, and fear. When these crop up, we ask God at once to remove them. We discuss them with someone immediately ....* Here is the repetition of Steps 4 and 5, 6 and 7, no longer undertaken as a major work but done routinely, continuously, as part of our everyday lives. We are discussing our thoughts and feelings with another person, another person who is qualified to discuss these matters because he or she is ....

Because he or she is *what?*

Well, no description at all is given of that person's qualifications, although from the context it appears that this is someone who is prepared to listen and presumably remain close-mouthed. *There is no indication that it is someone from who we should seek advice.* And we find a similar absence of any such description in the Big Book's treatment of Step 11. There, we read the following recommendation: *When we retire at night, we constructively review our day. Were we resentful, selfish, dishonest or afraid? Do we owe an apology? Have we kept something to ourselves which should be discussed with another person at once?* Who is this other person? Well, it might be a person we have wronged. But the phrasing suggests that this is a discussion with someone with whom we can share a confidence, someone like the person mentioned in Step 10 ... *someone, in fact, exactly like the person with whom we did our Fifth Step.*

If we reflect for a moment on the practice of Step 5 as recommended by the AA Big Book, and the treatment of Step 10 and Step 11 as outlined above, we will probably be struck by the lack of need in our recovery for any *experts* in our lives. Apparently Step 5 can be done perfectly adequately with someone who is not a sponsor, someone who is not even in Program. Apparently Step 10 can be done perfectly adequately with someone who is not a sponsor, someone who is not even in Program. And the same observation applies to Step 11. *In all three cases, the Big Book is talking about us having a "discussion."* In Step 5, it's a discussion of "our whole life story." In Step 10, it's a discussion of our selfishness, dishonesty, resentment, and fear. In Step 11, it's a discussion of something that we'd prefer to keep to ourselves. *But these are not discussions with "experts" in Program.* And if that's the case, *these discussions can't involve the asking for and the giving of advice.*

And there is another important observation we should make here. These discussions with "someone" or "another person" that take place in Step 10 and Step 11 are not discussions that are taking place for the first time in our recovery. Instead, they are a *repeat* of a discussion that first took place in Step 5: that discussion of our whole life story with a "partner." The sharing of our fears with another person in Step 10, and our revealing of information which we would rather keep to ourselves in Step 11, are a *continuation* of something that happened in Step 5 ... or at least, *they would be a continuation of what happened in Step 5 if we did our Step 5 the way the AA Big Book suggests it should be done.*

Let's go over that point once more. Steps 10 and 11 are in part a repetition of what happened in Step 5. The Big Book recommended that we discussed our whole life story with someone in Step 5. It recommends discussing ourselves with a similar person in Steps 10 and 11. The concept of *discussion* with someone who is wise and discreet, someone who may share his or her experience, someone who will not give advice, is central to all three Steps. But the Big Book recommends that this practice should begin in Step 5, with a discussion of our whole life story.

And now a major question presents itself. We have just seen that Steps 5, 10, and 11 are based in part on discussions. If, as we have suggested, in these discussions we are not supposed to receive any advice, *how are we going to determine what we are to do?* And that is the subject of the next chapter.

4. Our Higher Power

Admitted to God, to ourselves, and to another human being the exact nature of our wrongs.

-- Big Book, p.59

Observant readers of this *Guide* will already have noticed a conspicuous absentee from our short discussions of Steps 5, 10, and 11. And that absentee is our Higher Power.

Step 5 of Program reads, *Admitted to God, to ourselves, and to another human being the exact nature of our wrongs,* and so far we have paid little attention to the role of our Higher Power in our workings of these three Steps. It is important to see that we have omitted something very significant, because in both Step 5 and Step 10 our Higher Power is mentioned *first*. Step 5 begins, *Admitted to God* .... Step 10 says, *When [selfishness, dishonesty, resentment, and fear] crop up, we ask God at once to remove them.* In both cases, our relationship with our Higher Power comes first. The presence of another person is necessary in both Steps, but the interaction with our Higher Power is more important.

Not only is it important, *it is critical.* Even people in Program with many years of recovery can believe that our recovery is based primarily on our relationship with other people in Program. But that is not the primary basis of our recovery. The primary basis is our relationship with our Higher Power. In Step 2, in Step 3, in Step 5, in Steps 6 and 7, and in Step 10, that relationship with our Higher Power is either the only focus or the main focus. In Step 11, indeed, it *is* the *only* focus.

So it follows in Step 5 that when we tell our whole life story to another person, when we discuss that story with that person, we are also – as the Step phrases it – *admitting to God ... the exact nature of our wrongs.* We are not merely being honest for the first time in our lives with another person. We are being honest with God, with our Higher Power. No matter how close our relationship may be with the person to whom we are telling this story, unless we have at least some notion that we are simultaneously sharing this story with a Higher Power, our Step 5 may be less effective than it should be.

And a similar observation can be made about Step 10. We turn first to our Higher Power, then to someone else. The story we told in Step 5 to our Higher Power becomes the basis of an ongoing relationship to that Power. Step 10 urges us to make that relationship *routine.* Whenever we find we are selfish, dishonest, resentful, or afraid, we *routinely* ask God as we understand God at once to remove it, and we do that *first.* We don't talk to someone else first. We don't raise it as a topic in a 12-Step discussion meeting first. We don't make amends first. We don't resolutely turn our thoughts to someone we can help first. What we do first is this: we ask our Higher Power to remove it. And we do this *routinely.*

When we live our lives in this way, Step 11 almost takes care of itself. If we abandon our dependence on our willpower in Step 10 – and that is the main purpose of Step 10 – then learning to depend on intuition and inspiration, to depend on our Higher Power to direct our thinking in Step 11 becomes almost automatic. Every time we do this, every time we admit in Step 10 that we are upset and that we do not know what to do to correct that, every time we seek inspiration and direction from our Higher Power in Step 11, we are remembering what happened in Step 5. We are remembering that we told our whole life story, the new story that our Step 4 inventory had made possible, not only to another person but to God as we understood God. When we are completely honest and open with someone, we experience a closeness to that person. When we are completely open and honest with our Higher Power in Step 5, that creates a similar closeness with God as we understand God. Steps 10 and 11 are a further exploration of that closeness on a moment-by-moment basis. A relationship first explored in Step 5 starts to become *routine*.

5. Conclusion

A wise man used to go into a certain part of the forest to meditate. There he would light a fire, and say a special prayer, and God would make all well.

Many years after his death, his disciple went to the forest too. He had forgotten the ritual of lighting the fire, but he recited the special prayer, and God made all well.

A long time after that, his disciple repeated the practice. He had forgotten the prayer, but he was in the right part of the forest, and God made all well.

And many years afterwards, that man's disciple sat at home and said: "God, I have forgotten the fire ritual, I have forgotten the prayer, and I do not even know where to go in the forest. All I can do is tell you my story."

And God made all well, because God loves stories.

-- Traditional Jewish, modified

Lord, Thou knowest how busy I must be this day; if I forget Thee, do not Thou forget me.

-- Prayer of Sir Jacob Astley

When he had failed in his duty, he only confessed his fault, saying to God, "I shall never do otherwise, if You leave me to myself; 'tis You must hinder my falling, and mend what is amiss."

-- Brother Lawrence, "The Practice of the Presence of God"

What is it that the three quotes above have in common?

In each case, the person quoted is being honest about his story, and he is telling that story to God as he understands God. The second quote is supposedly the prayer that Sir Jacob Astley prayed before the Battle of Edgehill, in the English Civil War. Brother Lawrence worked in a monastery, but he was not a monk. For some reason, he was not able to achieve that: some traditions assert that he suffered from mental or emotional problems, but whatever the reason, he spent his life working in the monastery kitchens. It was not a life he cared for very much, but with the help of what we would call Step 10 he was contented, as his unusual prayer suggests.

Step 4 is the key that opens the door to a moment-by-moment relationship with our Higher Power. Our honest self-appraisal in Step 4, our realization that our lives as practicing addicts were governed by fear, enables us to tell our whole life story openly and honestly to God and another person in Step 5, and lays the foundation for a *routine* relationship with our Higher Power in Steps 10 and 11. And that relationship is built on the story that we are able to tell for the first time in Step 5 ... *if we do our Fifth Step as the Big Book recommends.*

What can we do if we are well advanced in our recovery but did our Fifth Step by reading our Step 4 inventory to another person? Well, doing our Fifth Step in this way will have done us no harm. But we may find enormous benefit from repeating our Fifth Step, not by reading an old or a new written inventory, but by practicing it *in just the way the Big Book recommends.* As was suggested earlier in this little *Guide,* many of us find significant benefit from *discussing our whole life story* with a person who is wise, humble, and close-mouthed.

You may wish to try it for yourself: you too may find that such a Fifth Step forms a natural foundation for the ongoing practice of Steps 10 and 11.

37079209R00022